TRUE HOPE

BREAK FREE FROM EMPTY PROMISES AND
TRANSFORM YOUR LIFE

ROBEL TEKLOM

Copyright © 2025 Brimlight Press.
All rights reserved.

No part of this book may be reproduced, stored, or transmitted in any form without written permission from the publisher, except in the case of brief quotations for reviews.

Scripture Quotations: Scripture quotations are taken from the World English Bible (WEB), which is in the public domain.

Brimlight Press
Website: www.brimlightpress.com
Email: brimlightpress@gmail.com

ISBN: 978-0-6483643-6-8

Acknowledgment

First and foremost, I give glory to God for His wisdom, guidance, and strength throughout this journey.

I would like to express my heartfelt gratitude to Lula Asgede for her invaluable time and effort in proofreading this book and offering thoughtful recommendations for improvement.

A special thanks to my wife, Ariam Kibrab, for her unwavering support, love, and encouragement along the way.

Table of Contents

Introduction 1

    My Journey to True Hope 2
    Why This Book Matters 3
    How to Engage with This Book 4
    What to Expect on This Journey 5

Chapter 1: Unveiling False Hopes 7

    The Allure of False Hope 7
    Where False Hope Begins 8
    Identifying False Hopes in Your Life 9
    Why We Cling to False Hopes 14
    The Hidden Cost of Temporary Comfort 17
    Breaking Free by Embracing Truth 18

Chapter 2: Discovering True Hope 20

    What Is True Hope? 20
    What It Means to Embrace True Hope 26
    The Challenges of Finding True Hope 29
    Self-Reflection Activity: 32
    Restoring the Heart and Mind 34
    The Impact of Hope 37
    Self-Reflection Activity: 40

Chapter 3: Living In True Hope 42

    Healing and Renewal Through Hope 44
    A Future Filled with Possibility 46
    Unshakable Love That Never Fades 48
    Finding Lasting Peace and Joy 50
    Forgiveness: The Key to Freedom 52
    A Hope That Goes Beyond This Life 54

    Sustained by God: Strength, Protection, and Victory 57
    Guidance for the Journey Ahead 60
    Wisdom and Resilience in Uncertain Times 62
    The Comfort of Knowing You're Never Alone 64

Chapter 4: True Hope in Action 69
    Making True Hope a Lifelong Foundation 69
    Daily Practices to Strengthen Hope 71
    Overcoming Doubt and Setbacks 73
    Finding True Hope in Uncertain Times 76
    True Hope-Filled Influence 77

Chapter 5: True Stories of Transformation 82
    Overcoming Life's Hardest Moments 82
    The Power of One Hopeful Heart 93

Chapter 6: Your Hope Journey 99
    Your Hope Reflections 99
    When Hope Feels Hard 101
    Identifying & Letting Go of False Hope 102
    Staying Anchored in True Hope Through Challenges .. 104
    Hope Practices Toolbox 107
    A Three-Step Action Plan 108
    Walking Forward with Confidence 111
    Where to Next? 112

Conclusion 115
    Key Takeaways from This Journey 115
    Living with Purpose and Confidence 117
    Step Into True Hope 118
    My Hope Commitment 123
    About the Author 124

Introduction

Welcome to "True Hope"

Before we begin, I want to take a moment to share why I wrote this book and how you can get the most out of it.

We all reach moments in life where we ask deep questions: *Is there more to this life? Is there something unshakable I can hold onto?* Maybe you've placed your hope in something or someone, only to be disappointed. Maybe you feel stuck, uncertain, or even hopeless. If that resonates with you, I want you to know this: You are not alone.

This book is not about quick-fix motivation or feel-good positivity. It's about discovering true, lasting hope, hope that remains firm even when life is uncertain.

If you have ever searched for that kind of hope, then this book is for you.

My Journey to True Hope

Like many, I once placed my trust in things that seemed secure, success, health, relationships, and personal goals, only to realize that when life took an unexpected turn, those things couldn't sustain me.

I remember the sleepless nights, the weight of anxiety, and the racing thoughts. *What if I never get better? What if my struggles consume me completely?* My mental health was deteriorating, affecting every area of my life. I felt trapped in a cycle of stress and self-doubt.

In that place of deep searching, someone guided me toward a discovery that changed everything. I pray this book becomes an open door for you, one that leads you to the same life-changing hope.

This hope brought clarity where there was confusion, peace where there was anxiety, and purpose where there was uncertainty. It wasn't tied to circumstances or achievements; it remained unshakable.

That's why I wrote this book.

I don't just want to tell you, my story; I want to invite you into your own journey of discovery. As you turn these pages, I pray you will recognise where you've placed your trust, release false hopes, and embrace the only hope that truly lasts.

Perhaps you're wondering: *What makes this hope different? How can I be sure it won't fail me?*

That's exactly what we're going to explore together.

Why This Book Matters

This isn't just about understanding true hope, it's about experiencing and living in it.

Too often, hope is defined as a feeling of optimism, a positive outlook, or the belief that things will get better. And while those things are good, they aren't enough.

True hope isn't mere optimism; it is unwavering, even in life's uncertainties.

This book will help you:

- Evaluate where you've placed your hope, does it sustain you, or is it holding you back from something real?
- Discover a hope strong enough to carry you through all phases of life.

More than words on a page, this is an experience, a journey that will challenge, encourage, and guide you toward a new way of seeing hope.

As you read, keep this in mind: hope isn't just something we cling to, it's something that carries us through.

How to Engage with This Book

To get the most out of this book, engage with it fully. Some ideas may challenge you. They may ask you to rethink certain beliefs or confront difficult emotions. But that's where real growth happens.

Throughout these chapters, you'll find:

- Self-reflection questions to help you examine your own experiences.
- Personal reflections and experiences from those who have walked their own hope journeys.
- Practical steps to apply what you are learning, helping you not just understand hope, but actively walk in it daily.

Take your time. Pause when needed. Reflect on the questions. Be honest with yourself.

Above all, stay open to the possibility that there is genuine, transformative and lasting hope available to you, more than you may have imagined.

What to Expect on This Journey

This book will guide you toward a hope that is strong, enduring, and unshakable.

- First, we'll uncover false hopes, the things we often rely on, like success, people, or financial security, only to find they cannot sustain us when life gets difficult.

- Then, we'll explore true hope, what it is, why it's different from the substitutes we often chase and how it changes everything.

- Finally, you'll hear powerful testimonies from people who have experienced real transformation through the power of true hope.

By the end of this journey, my prayer is that you will:

- Let go of false hopes.
- Discover and embrace true, lasting hope.
- Learn to live in that hope daily, even in uncertainty.
- Be inspired to share this hope with others.

This is your journey. Take a deep breath, open your heart, and get ready.

Let's begin.

Chapter 1: Unveiling False Hopes

The Allure of False Hope

Hope is a fundamental part of human existence. It drives us to persevere, to dream, and to seek meaning in life. However, not all hopes are built on solid ground. More often than not, we find ourselves chasing after illusions, false hopes that promise security, fulfillment, or success but ultimately fail to satisfy.

In times of hardship, people naturally seek quick solutions and emotional relief. False hope is enticing because it offers what we crave most: control, comfort, and certainty.

False hope can take many forms:

- The belief that success or wealth will bring lasting fulfillment.
- The idea that another person will "complete" us.
- The expectation that external circumstances will fix internal struggles.

At first, these promises seem logical and achievable. But why do they always feel just out of reach? The answer lies in where false hopes originate and how they continue to shape our thinking today.

Where False Hope Begins

The tendency to chase after false hope is not a modern phenomenon. It is something that has been part of the human experience since the very beginning.

In Genesis 3, we see this play out in the story of Adam and Eve. When the serpent deceived them, he did not offer them something obviously harmful. Instead, he promised something enticing, the chance to be like God, to possess greater knowledge, to be in control. It was a false hope, wrapped in the illusion of wisdom and power.

Despite God's clear command, they trusted their desires over the truth, leading to disillusionment, brokenness, and separation from their Creator. What they thought would bring fulfillment led only to suffering.

This moment in history established a pattern that persists today. People have long sought fulfillment in wealth, relationships, and success, convinced these will bring lasting satisfaction. Yet, even when their desires are met, a longing for something more remains.

Identifying False Hopes in Your Life

False hopes promise relief and security, but they always fall short. Here are some of the most common false hopes people chase:

Material Success: Many believe that wealth, possessions, or career achievements will bring lasting happiness. They set financial goals, chase promotions, or build businesses, convinced that security and fulfillment lie in success. While financial stability is beneficial, it does not satisfy the soul's deeper needs. Many who achieve wealth still experience emptiness, proving that material success is not the key to lasting joy.

Relationships: People often expect a spouse, family, or friendships to provide the fulfillment they seek. They believe that if they find the right person or maintain deep social connections, they will never feel alone or unfulfilled. Relationships are valuable but cannot fully satisfy our need for identity, security, or worth. Depending on others for fulfillment can lead to disappointment, co-dependency, or heartbreak.

Self-Sufficiency/Self-Reliance: Many trust in their own strength, intelligence, or discipline to navigate life's challenges. They believe that if they plan well, work hard, and make the right decisions, they can secure their future and control their destiny. Independence is often seen as the highest ideal, believing that needing help is a sign of weakness.

While diligence and wisdom are valuable, life is unpredictable. Unexpected hardships, such as illness, financial downturns, or personal loss, can disrupt even the most well-prepared plans. Relying solely on oneself often leads to anxiety, exhaustion, and isolation. True security is not found in personal strength, as self-sufficiency has its limits.

Escapism: Instead of confronting life's challenges, many turn to distractions such as:

- Substance abuse (drugs, alcohol, smoking, or other addictive substances)
- Constant travel (using movement as an escape rather than genuine exploration)
- Screen addiction (excessive social media, binge-watching, or online engagement)
- Fantasy and fiction (immersing in books, movies, or TV to avoid present struggles)
- Daydreaming (imagining a better future without taking real action)
- False spiritual or shamanic practices (seeking power or peace through deception)
- Workaholism (burying oneself in work to suppress emotional pain)
- Extreme sports and thrill-seeking (pursuing danger for an adrenaline escape)
- Food and cooking (emotional eating as a coping mechanism)
- Nature and outdoor activities (turning adventure into an escape rather than enjoyment)
- Art and creativity (using expression as a shield from deeper struggles)

- Socializing, parties, and entertainment (using events, music, and crowds to numb emotions and detach from reality)
- Shopping and retail therapy (buying unnecessary things for momentary excitement)
- Virtual reality and gaming (immersing in artificial worlds to avoid personal challenges)
- Excessive sleep (retreating into sleep to escape life's demands)

Music, art, travel, and nature are gifts from God, meant to bring joy and inspiration. However, when they become a means of escape rather than a path to true healing, they can lead to stagnation. Lasting transformation doesn't come through avoidance but by confronting and addressing deeper struggles.

Nostalgia: Some believe that happiness only existed in the past. They romanticize "the good old days," convinced that life was better back then. Clinging to the past prevents growth. Focusing on what was, instead of what is, leads to discontentment and missed opportunities.

Politics and Social Movements: Many hope that a perfect political leader, system, or social reform will solve all problems. While policy changes can improve circumstances, they cannot change the human heart. True transformation cannot come from external systems alone.

Revenge or Justice: Some believe that receiving an apology, winning an argument, or seeing justice served will bring them peace. Even if justice is achieved, bitterness remains unless true healing takes place. Freedom comes not from revenge but from forgiveness.

Health and Fitness: Society glorifies physical appearance, youth, and fitness, leading many to believe that achieving the perfect body will bring lasting confidence. Aging is inevitable. Beauty and physical ability fade, but identity rooted in something deeper is unshakable.

Science and Technology: Some trust in human innovation, medicine, and artificial intelligence to provide ultimate solutions. While science improves lives, it cannot fulfill the soul's longing for purpose, morality, or meaning.

Superstition and Mysticism: Many seek guidance from horoscopes, tarot readings, manifestation, or rituals to gain control over their destiny. These practices provide a false sense of security but lack any real foundation. Truth is not something we create; it is something we discover and embrace.

When false hopes fail, they leave us searching for something deeper. Yet, despite disappointment, many still hold onto them.

Why We Cling to False Hopes

Even after false hopes disappoint us, we often refuse to let them go. Rather than accepting their failure, we grip them tighter, convinced that just a little more effort will change the outcome. But why?

The Illusion of Control: Many people resist true hope because it requires surrender. Society glorifies independence, teaching personal autonomy as life's greatest pursuit. This deception mirrors the temptation in the story of Adam and Eve, where autonomy became humanity's downfall. Accepting true hope means letting go of self-sufficiency and trusting God.

The Fear of Uncertainty: False hope creates an illusion of stability. People would rather cling to unreliable things than face the unknown, because at least their illusion feels familiar. Just as Adam and Eve grasped for control, many today choose certainty, even when that certainty is a lie.

The Search for Validation and Identity: Society often equates success, relationships, and achievements with self-worth. People chase status or admiration to prove their value, fearing that without these things, they will have nothing left.

The Desire for Comfort and Familiarity: False hope often feels safe simply because it's what people have always known. Letting go would mean stepping into discomfort and transformation, which can feel overwhelming.

- People stay in toxic relationships because being alone feels scarier.
- Others chase unrealistic dreams because admitting failure is painful.
- Some continue harmful habits because breaking them feels unfamiliar.

The Illusion of Progress: False hope deceives people into believing they are making progress, even when they are only delaying the inevitable.

- "If I just try harder, this will change."
- "If I ignore the warning signs, everything will work out."
- "I've invested too much to quit now."

Society celebrates persistence but rarely questions whether the direction is right.

Avoiding Pain and Responsibility: False hope provides an escape from hard truths. Rather than taking action, people wait for luck, shift blame, or postpone responsibility. Rather than admitting mistakes, they blame others. Instead of making difficult choices, they postpone action. Instead of addressing problems, they seek quick fixes.

The Need for Immediate Relief: We live in a world that instant gratification. Clinging to false hope is often easier than enduring the slow process of real transformation.

- Rather than working through struggles, people seek quick emotional relief.
- Rather than healing, they distract themselves with entertainment, busyness, or surface-level solutions.

False hopes create the illusion of security, success, or happiness, but they always fall short. Though letting go is hard, clinging to them carries a hidden cost, one that often goes unnoticed until it's too late

The Hidden Cost of Temporary Comfort

Clinging to false hopes comes at a great cost, mentally, emotionally, and spiritually. When expectations fail to align with reality, disappointment, frustration, and regret take hold.

False hope creates instability, leading to anxiety from repeated disappointments, emptiness when superficial pursuits fail, and misplaced trust that weakens inner resilience.

Instead of confronting reality, many remain stuck in cycles of procrastination, waiting for breakthroughs that never come. Avoidance behaviors that hinder true growth. Dependency on others for validation, leading to strained relationships.

Chasing empty hopes not only leads to disappointment but also drains valuable time, energy, and resources. The longer we hold on, the more we risk burnout, financial strain, and missed opportunities for real transformation. But freedom begins when we shift our focus from what deceives to what truly sustains.

Breaking Free by Embracing Truth

Awareness of false hope's cost opens the door to true discernment and wisdom. This process is not merely about abandoning falsehoods but about discovering a deeper, more fulfilling truth that has been there all along. Pause for a moment and reflect on your own life and experiences:

- Are there aspirations, desires, or beliefs that resonate with the false hopes we've discussed?
- Are there areas where you may be clinging to false hopes without realising it?

- Imagine if you let go of a false hope today. How would your emotions, mindset, and daily life change? What would you gain in peace, clarity, or freedom?

By courageously confronting the false hopes we hold onto, we begin to see the world with fresh eyes. But what happens when everything we've relied on proves insufficient? Is there a hope that doesn't fail?

False hopes are like invisible chains, subtle yet strong. They bind the heart with empty promises and blind the eyes to what is real and lasting. These false hopes offer temporary comfort but never bring true peace. They distract, delay, and deceive, keeping individuals from recognizing the only true hope that can set them free.

Let's embark on this journey together, discovering true hope, not another illusion, but a hope with a foundation so firm that it can sustain us through all of life's uncertainties. If false hopes always fail, is there one that never does?

Chapter 2: Discovering True Hope

What Is True Hope?

Hope shapes our emotions, decisions, and how we approach the future. It is one of the most powerful forces in life. Many think of hope as a feeling of expectation, a wish for something better, or simple optimism. But true hope goes far deeper, it's an unshakable foundation that brings strength, stability, and assurance, even in life's toughest moments.

True hope is not just an anticipation of something good that is yet to come, it is deeply rooted in faith and trust in God's promises.

Romans 15:13 says, "*Now may the God of hope fill you with all joy and peace in believing, that you may abound in hope in the power of the Holy Spirit.*" This verse reminds us that true hope comes from God and is accompanied by joy and peace when we fully trust in Him.

Hope is also closely intertwined with faith. Hebrews 11:1 defines faith and its connection to hope: "*Now faith is assurance of things hoped for, proof of things not seen."* This means that hope is built upon the certainty of God's faithfulness, even when we do not yet see the fulfillment of His promises.

The Bible describes hope as an anchor for the soul, firm and secure (Hebrews 6:19), illustrating its ability to keep us steady when life feels unstable. Unlike worldly hope, which shifts with circumstances, true hope stands firm on the unwavering character of God and His promises.

Many people place their hope in things that appear reliable, financial security, relationships, career success, personal achievements, or social status. While these things may bring temporary stability, they are not lasting sources of hope. Wealth can disappear, relationships can fail, and success can be fleeting. When challenges arise, these forms of hope often collapse, leaving behind uncertainty and despair.

However, true hope does not depend on temporary conditions, it is built on something eternal and unbreakable. This hope does not fade when circumstances change, nor does it rely on human effort. It is a certainty that God's truth and faithfulness endure, offering security and peace no matter what we face.

True hope fortifies us in uncertainty, reassures us in loss, and sustains us in suffering. It does not dismiss or eliminate hardships but reshapes our experience of them, instilling the confidence to endure. Rooted in the assurance of a greater plan unfolding beyond our sight, this hope offers lasting peace that transcends external circumstances. It enables us to look beyond immediate struggles and trust in something far greater than ourselves.

Hope Found in Christ

The Bible teaches that true and lasting hope is found in Jesus Christ. 1 Peter 1:3 declares: "*Blessed be the God and Father of our Lord Jesus Christ, who according to his great mercy caused us to be born again to a living hope through the resurrection of Jesus Christ from the dead.*"

This verse reveals a profound truth: Hope is more than an idea or a momentary emotion, it's alive and active, shaping the way we live. While living according to God's Word requires our effort and obedience, true hope is not something we can attain through our own strength. It is not based on human effort or achievements but on the resurrection of Jesus Christ.

Because Jesus conquered sin and death, those who trust in Him receive a hope that does not fade, disappoint, or fail. And through this true hope, who is Christ, they are given the power, by His Spirit, to overcome sin in this life and, through Him, conquer death in the life to come.

Unlike human hope, which is often uncertain, hope in Christ is solid. Jesus is described as the hope of the world. *"Christ in you, the hope of glory."* (Colossians 1:27). This means that those who believe in Him do not have to depend on the instability of human solutions or temporary fixes. Instead, they can build their lives on the solid foundation, Jesus Christ.

Through His resurrection, Jesus offers hope beyond this life. One that guarantees redemption, restoration, and eternal life to those who trust in Him. This hope is not distant or theoretical; it is deeply personal and transformative. Worldly hope comes and goes with circumstances, but the hope

Christ gives is eternal, unbreakable, and anchored in God's faithfulness.

Romans 5:5 assures us: "*Hope doesn't disappoint us, because God's love has been poured into our hearts through the Holy Spirit who was given to us.*" This means that hope in Christ is not empty, it is a source of strength, renewal, and transformation.

More than a future promise, this hope changes how we live in the present. Romans 8:24-25 states: "*For we were saved in hope, but hope that is seen is not hope. For who hopes for that which he sees? But if we hope for that which we don't see, we wait for it with patience.*" Hope in Christ teaches us to wait with patience, trusting in God's unseen but certain promises.

The prophet Isaiah also speaks of this hope in Isaiah 40:31: "*But those who wait for the lord will renew their strength. They will mount up with wings like eagles. They will run, and not be weary. They will walk, and not faint.*" Hope in Christ strengthens us as we wait on Him, renewing our endurance and giving us the ability to persevere without growing weary.

This hope is not just a theological concept, it is practical and life-changing. It gives us a reason to press on when we feel overwhelmed and a foundation to stand on when everything around us is uncertain.

It is this living hope that enables us to find meaning in suffering, courage in uncertainty, and strength in weakness. It shifts our focus from temporary setbacks to the eternal promises of God. Because of Christ, hope is not a distant dream, it is a present reality.

This is the kind of hope that sustains us in the darkest of times and fills us with the assurance that no matter what happens, we are held by something far greater than ourselves. It is the kind of hope that can transform hearts, bring true healing, and give meaning to every part of our journey.

Hope in Christ is both a foundation that holds us firm and a path we choose to walk in. While God is our source of hope, we are called to actively respond by embracing it daily.

What It Means to Embrace True Hope

To embrace true hope is to trust in something greater than ourselves, to release temporary securities, and to step into the confidence that God's promises are true. Embracing true hope isn't about ignoring our struggles, but about standing firm; knowing that no challenge is meaningless, no failure is final, and no situation is beyond redemption.

Hebrews 10:23 encourages us: "*Let's hold fast the confession of our hope without wavering; for he who promised is faithful.*" This kind of hope does not remove difficulties, but it is anchored in God's faithfulness, giving us the strength to endure without wavering, even in difficult times.

Romans 15:13 conveys the message that God, as the source of hope, fills those who trust in Him with deep joy and peace. This assurance allows believers to experience an overflowing sense of hope, not through their own efforts, but through the empowering presence of the Holy Spirit. It emphasizes that true hope is a divine gift, not something we must create on our own.

True hope also shapes our present actions. It does not lead to passivity but calls us to live with faith, courage, and purpose. To live in hope means:

- To persevere through hardship, knowing that trials refine us and build character (James 1:2-4).
- To trust in God's plans, understanding that He is working for our good, even when we don't see the full picture.
- To live with peace, resting in the assurance that God is faithful and will never abandon us.
- To walk in purpose, aligning our lives with truth rather than temporary pursuits.
- To find strength in God's Word, allowing Scripture to guide and sustain us when doubt rise.
- To cultivate patience and endurance, understanding that God's promises unfold in His perfect timing.

The Bible reminds us that hope is not shallow; it is a firm assurance rooted in something greater. Jeremiah 29:11 declares: "*For I know the thoughts that I think toward you," says Yahweh, "thoughts of peace, and not of evil, to give you hope and a future.*" This promise speaks to God's intentional care, reminding us that even in uncertainty, He is leading us toward a greater purpose.

Hope also enables us to encourage others. 2 Corinthians 1:3-4 says: "*Blessed be the God and Father of our Lord Jesus Christ, the Father of mercies and God of all comfort, who comforts us in all our affliction, that we may be able to comfort those who are in any affliction, through the comfort with which we ourselves are comforted by God.*" When we embrace true hope, we are equipped to share it with those who are struggling.

As we continue exploring what it means to walk in this hope, may we open our hearts to the truth that true hope is not something to wish for, it is something to live in. It is the foundation upon which we build our faith, the assurance that no matter what we face, we are never without purpose, never without a future, and never without the love of God.

The Challenges of Finding True Hope

While true hope is available and close to us all, many people struggle to find it. Various obstacles, both internal and external, can make it difficult to embrace hope in a meaningful and lasting way. Understanding these challenges can help us recognise what stands in the way and take steps toward experiencing the deep and unwavering hope that God offers.

Pride: Ego and self-reliance can be significant barriers to seeking true hope. Many believe they must rely solely on their own abilities, wisdom, or success to navigate life's challenges. This mindset often leads people to place trust in the temporary rather than acknowledging their dependence on God. Pride prevents individuals from surrendering to God's will and embracing the enduring, lasting hope He provides.

Spiritual Warfare: The Bible acknowledges the presence of spiritual opposition that seeks to hinder people from discovering true hope. Spiritual warfare can manifest as doubt, confusion, or persistent struggles that make it difficult to trust in God's promises. These opposing forces work to deceive and keep individuals trapped in fear, discouragement, or disbelief.

Emotional and Mental Struggles: Pain, loss, and hardship can make true hope feel out of reach, leading to despair and doubt. Mental health issues and emotional wounds can cloud a person's ability to see hope, leading them to question whether true hope is even possible.

Past Disappointments and Pain: For many, past disappointments create an emotional barrier to hope. Those who have faced betrayals, failures, or shattered dreams may struggle to trust again, fearing more pain. The scars of past hardships can prevent individuals from believing that true hope exists, leading them to adopt a defensive, skeptical outlook on life.

Uncertainty About the Future: Fear of what lies ahead can prevent individuals from embracing true hope. Anxiety about what may happen in the future, financial struggles, illness, failure, or other uncertainties, can overwhelm people, making them hesitant to trust in anything beyond their immediate control.

Fear of Vulnerability: Embracing hope requires trust, and trust often requires vulnerability. Many resist hope because they fear being let down. It can feel safer to remain skeptical than to risk believing in something that may not turn out as expected. However, this guarded mindset can keep people from experiencing the full peace that true hope offers.

Seeking Hope in the Wrong Places: Many seek fulfillment in success, relationships, material possessions, or temporary pleasures, only to find that these things do not provide lasting hope. This endless pursuit of false security leaves individuals feeling empty and searching for something more substantial.

Influence of Society and Culture: Biblical hope often goes against the tide of popular opinion. Society promotes instant gratification, self-reliance, and personal ambition over faith in something greater. This cultural pressure can make it difficult for individuals to pursue true hope without feeling out of place or ridiculed.

Despite these challenges, seeking genuine living hope is a rewarding and transformative endeavor. Through humility, faith in God, Scripture, and prayer, individuals can overcome these obstacles and experience the fullness of hope found in God's promises.

Self-Reflection Activity:

Take a moment to reflect on your own life and identify any challenges or obstacles you have faced in seeking genuine hope and meaning. Consider the following:

- Moments of doubt, fear, or uncertainty that may have hindered your sense of hope.

- The role that ego has played in your pursuit of living hope. Have feelings of pride, self-reliance, or entitlement ever gotten in the way of your ability to trust in something greater than yourself? Reflect on how ego may have influenced your attitudes and actions.

- Describe a time when an outside force (e.g., society, culture, or a personal hardship) challenged your ability to hold onto hope.

How did you respond, and what did you learn from it?

- Reflect on the concept of spiritual warfare and how it relates to your own experiences. Have you ever felt like you were battling against unseen forces or internal struggles that threatened your faith and hope? How did you respond to these challenges?

- Think about the strategies you have used to cope with challenges in seeking hope. Have these strategies been effective, or do they tend to perpetuate feelings of hopelessness or despair? Consider whether there are healthier ways to approach difficult situations and cultivate a sense of hope.

- Finally, set intentions for how you can overcome challenges and cultivate living hope in your life.

Remember, self-reflection is an ongoing process, and it's okay to revisit these questions periodically as you continue to navigate your journey towards living hope.

Restoring the Heart and Mind

True hope, the hope found in God, offers a transformative power that extends beyond mere optimism. It is grounded in the unchanging promises of God, who is faithful, sovereign, and full of love. This hope serves as an anchor, providing stability even in times of suffering, uncertainty, and adversity.

While temporary hope fades with changing circumstances, genuine hope offers an eternal perspective. It shifts our focus beyond present struggles, reminding us that true security lies in God's promises of redemption and eternal life. Hebrews 6:19 describes hope as "*an anchor of the soul, a hope both sure and steadfast,*" emphasizing its ability to hold us steady even in life's storms.

In moments of hardship, true hope provides more than comfort, it reassures us that we are never alone, that God walks with us through our trials, offering His grace and mercy. Isaiah 41:10 reminds us of this: "*Don't you be afraid, for I am with you. Don't be dismayed, for I am your God. I will strengthen you. Yes, I will help you. Yes, I will uphold you with the right hand of my righteousness.*"

Beyond its role in endurance, genuine hope also inspires a life of righteousness and faithfulness. It motivates us to pursue holiness, knowing that our lives are part of a bigger picture and that our faith is not in vain. Titus 2:11-13 encourages believers to live godly lives while looking forward to the "*blessed hope and appearing of the glory of our great God and Savior, Jesus Christ*."

Furthermore, genuine hope fosters resilience. It helps us trust in God's providence, believing that He is working all things together for good, even when circumstances seem bleak. This assurance transforms our mindset, allowing us to remain steadfast, not easily shaken by life's uncertainties.

God calls us to be resilient, not in our own strength, but through dependence on Him. Our perseverance is an act of faith, taking steps forward while trusting that He guides and sustains us.

Hope in God is not just about the future, it shapes how we live today. It gives meaning to our pain, purpose to our actions, and peace in the face of trials. It is this hope that brings healing to the heart and mind, renewing our spirits and allowing us to experience lasting joy in God's presence.

A powerful biblical example of this truth Is Job.

Job was a man who experienced immense suffering, he lost his wealth, his health, and even his children. His body was afflicted with painful sores, and his closest friends accused him of wrongdoing. In the midst of his suffering, he wrestled with deep questions, crying out to God in his anguish. Yet, despite his pain and confusion, Job never completely lost hope in God.

In Job 19:25-26, he declares: *"But as for me, I know that my Redeemer lives. In the end, he will stand upon the earth. After my skin is destroyed, then I will see God in my flesh."*

This statement reveals Job's enduring hope, not only for deliverance in his lifetime but in the ultimate promise of redemption and resurrection. Even though his present circumstances seemed unbearable, his hope in God shaped his response to suffering. Instead of turning away, he persevered in faith, trusting in God's justice and sovereignty.

In the end, God healed and restored Job, blessing him with more than he had before (Job 42:10-17). But more importantly, Job's spiritual understanding was deepened, and his relationship with God was strengthened. His hope led him through pain, gave him purpose amid trials, and ultimately renewed his spirit.

Job's story illustrates that hope in God is not just about the future, it transforms how we endure hardships today. It gives meaning to suffering, strengthens our faith, and allows us to experience peace even when life is uncertain.

The Impact of Hope

Hope shapes how we endure life's challenges. Without it, deep emotional and spiritual struggles arise. When hope is not grounded in Christ, people seek fulfillment in places that ultimately leave them empty.

The Devastating Effects of Hopelessness

Without an ultimate sense of purpose, individuals may experience:
- A lingering emptiness, feeling that nothing is ever enough
- Chronic anxiety over the future and fear of the unpredictable
- Depression stemming from a lack of confidence that suffering has meaning
- Identity confusion and low self-worth, driven by external validation
- Unhealthy coping mechanisms that provide only temporary relief
- Difficulty with forgiveness, leading to bitterness and strained relationships
- Moral and emotional instability, wrestling with right and wrong in the absence of God's truth

Many attempt to escape their pain through distractions, yet these provide only fleeting relief, deepening their struggles over time. Without Christ, identity becomes tied to shifting worldly standards, leading to exhaustion and insecurity.

The Transformative Power of True Hope in Christ

Unlike fleeting worldly hope, true hope in Christ is unwavering and life-changing. It provides:
- A meaningful life rooted in God's greater purpose
- A peace that transcends understanding, regardless of circumstances
- Strength to endure suffering with confidence, knowing God is in control

Rather than striving for approval or fearing rejection, those who trust in Christ rest in the assurance that they are loved, chosen, and redeemed. This newfound identity replaces insecurity and fear with contentment and confidence.

Healing and Renewal Through Faith

Hope in Christ renews the mind, heals emotional wounds, and provides strength to forgive and love freely. Instead of being bound by past hurts, believers walk in the freedom of God's grace, experiencing true healing, mentally, emotionally, and spiritually.

With Christ, suffering is no longer meaningless. It becomes an opportunity for growth, refining faith rather than breaking it. By anchoring their hope in God's unchanging truth, believers gain the resilience to face life's challenges with peace and assurance.

Self-Reflection Activity:

Take a moment to reflect on your personal journey with hope. Consider the following questions:

- Where do I currently place my hope, and how does it affect my sense of peace, purpose, and emotional well-being?

- Have I experienced anxiety, fear, or hopelessness in areas of my life? How might placing my trust in Christ change the way I respond to these struggles?

- How do I respond to suffering and difficult circumstances? Do I see them as meaningless hardships, or do I believe that God can use them for a greater purpose?

- What would my life look like if my hope was anchored in something eternal rather than in temporary circumstances?

Hope in Christ is not just a belief, it's a reality that transforms every part of life. Those who embrace it find peace, healing, and a deep assurance that nothing in this world can shake.

But how do we live in this hope daily? In the next chapter, we'll explore practical ways to make this hope our foundation, shaping our thoughts, guiding our actions, and strengthening our relationships.

Chapter 3: Living In True Hope

Hope holds us securely, but we must also choose to hold onto it, trusting, believing, and living in its truth. True hope is both a gift and a commitment.

Hope is not just something we reach for, it holds us fast, sustaining us through life's trials. While we are called to trust and hold onto hope, it is ultimately hope itself, rooted in God's unshakable faithfulness, that carries us, even when our grip falters.

There will be moments when challenges feel insurmountable and our faith wavers, but true hope does not rely on our strength alone. It rests on the unwavering promises of God, steady and sure. Numbers 23:19 reminds us, "*God is not a man, that he should lie, nor a son of man, that he should repent. Has he said, and he won't do it? Or has he spoken, and he won't make it good*".

Living in true hope means anchoring our confidence in God, not in fleeting circumstances. It means trusting in His timing, relying on His wisdom, and resting in the certainty of His love. When we embrace true hope, we find the courage to persevere, the faith to stand firm, and the peace that surpasses all understanding.

We are called to trust in God's promises but even when we struggle, His faithfulness never wavers. He will always keep His word, and that is why true hope is not fragile or fleeting, it is steadfast, rooted in the very character of God.

Philippians 1:6 reassures us, "*Being confident of this, that he who began a good work in you will carry it on to completion until the day of Christ Jesus.*" This verse offers a powerful assurance; once we begin a journey of faith with God, He is committed to finishing the work He started in us.

Living in true hope means trusting that our future is secure in God's hands. Even when the road ahead seems uncertain, we can rest in the truth that He is working in and through us. True hope doesn't just change our perspective; it transforms us from within. As we hold onto this hope, we are also held by it, renewed daily and continually shaped into the people God created us to be.

Let's explore what it truly means to live in this hope, how it brings healing, fills our future with possibility, provides resolute love, and grants wisdom and resilience in every season of life.

Healing and Renewal Through Hope

True hope heals the deepest wounds of our hearts and minds. Many carry past failures, regrets, and emotional scars, but God's hope brings renewal. Jeremiah 30:17 declares, *"For I will restore health to you, and I will heal you of your wounds, says Yahweh,"*

Often, people seek healing solely through their own efforts, neglecting to invite God into the process. This can lead to isolation, frustration, and limited progress.

Yet, the Bible assures us that God is faithful to His promises, including the promise of healing. When we anchor our healing journey in His word, we find strength, assurance, and the reminder that He is always with us in this journey.

Living in true hope means recognising that healing is often a journey. However, in some cases, God may grant instant healing when it is the only option for that person, for nothing is impossible for Him. God walks with us every step, restoring broken hearts, renewing weary souls, and bringing peace to anxious minds. *"He heals the broken in heart, and binds up their wounds"* (Psalm 147:3).

True hope does not remove trials but gives us strength to endure them. It brings immediate peace even as we walk through long-term struggles, assuring us that our hardships have meaning and purpose in God's plan.

Hope is the bridge between brokenness and restoration, it keeps us moving forward even when healing feels slow or uncertain. To live in this hope means surrendering our pain to God, trusting that He will bring beauty from ashes. It is choosing faith over fear, believing in His plan for restoration, and experiencing healing daily through His grace, peace, and presence.

Self-Reflection Activity:
- How are you structuring your journey toward healing and recovery?
- Without involving the ultimate healer, do you believe genuine healing and recovery can be achieved?

A Future Filled with Possibility

True hope replaces fear with expectation. Even when the road is unclear, we can trust that God's plans are intentional and for our good. *"We know that all things work together for good for those who love God, for those who are called according to his purpose"* (Romans 8:28). Hope moves us forward, it reinforces our faith, helps us embrace change, and allows us to step into new opportunities with sureness in His plan.

Living in hope shifts our mindset from scarcity to abundance. Instead of dwelling on what we lack, we trust in God's provision: *"My God will supply every need of yours according to his riches in glory in Christ Jesus"* (Philippians 4:19). When we rely on Him, our choices are shaped by faith, not fear.

A future filled with possibility doesn't mean an easy path, but it does mean every step has purpose. Setbacks are not the end of the story; God is still writing it. *"Trust in Yahweh with all your heart, and don't lean on your own understanding. In all your ways acknowledge him, and he will make your paths straight"* (Proverbs 3:5-6).

To live in this hope is to walk forward, knowing that our future is not uncertain but secure in God's hands. It is waking up with expectation, believing that He is leading, opening doors, and guiding us into the fullness of His plan. Our confidence in the future isn't based on changing circumstances but on the unwavering faithfulness of God.

Self-Reflection Activity:
- Reflect on the plans you've made in the past and those you hold now.
- Have they ever offered you the same reassurance and confidence that God is promising?

Unshakable Love That Never Fades

Human love can waver, relationships shift, and circumstances challenge our sense of belonging. But God's love is steadfast and eternal, never dependent on our failures or the changes around us. Jeremiah 31:3 declares, *"Yes, I have loved you with an everlasting love. Therefore, I have drawn you with loving kindness."* His love remains constant, unwavering, and unshaken.

Paul reinforces this in Romans 8:38-39: *"For I am persuaded that neither death, nor life, nor angels, nor principalities, nor things present, nor things to come, nor powers, nor height, nor depth, nor any other created thing will be able to separate us from God's love which is in Christ Jesus our Lord."* Can you imagine, nothing physical or spiritual, can sever us from His deep and abiding love.

Isaiah 54:10 further assures us: *"For the mountains may depart, and the hills be removed, but my loving kindness will not depart from you, and my covenant of peace will not be removed."* Life's uncertainties do not alter His faithfulness. No matter how unstable life feels, no matter who has walked away or what has crumbled around you, God's love remains. His faithfulness is unshaken, His peace unbreakable. You are not forgotten; you are held by the One whose love will never leave you.

If you have never heard the words 'I love you' from those who should have cherished you, if love has felt distant or conditional in your life, know this: God's love for you is everlasting and unshaken, and in His love, there is unshakable hope. But to experience the depth of this love and hope, you must acknowledge and receive it.

True hope rests in knowing we are fully known, deeply loved, and never abandoned. 1 John 4:10 reminds us, *"In this is love, not that we loved God, but that he loved us, and sent his Son as the atoning sacrifice for our sins."* Rooted in His love, we are free to love without fear, forgive freely, and embrace our identity as His children.

Psalm 136:1 calls us to gratitude: *"Give thanks to Yahweh, for he is good, for his loving kindness endures forever."* Living in this hope means not just trusting in His love but rejoicing in it, standing firm in the unshakable foundation of His everlasting love.

Self-Reflection Activity:
- Write a letter to yourself about a time when you felt deeply loved. How did it impact your sense of worth and security? If you haven't experienced such love, what would it mean for you to receive it?
- Do you genuinely believe there is someone in your life capable of loving you with an everlasting love?

Finding Lasting Peace and Joy

God's peace and joy are not tied to circumstances but are deeply rooted in His presence.

Philippians 4:7 assures, *"And the peace of God, which surpasses all understanding, will guard your hearts and your thoughts in Christ Jesus."* This divine peace steadies the soul even in uncertainty. Jesus confirmed this in John 14:27: *"Peace I leave with you. My peace I give to you; not as the world gives, I give to you. Don't let your heart be troubled, neither let it be fearful."* Unlike the fleeting peace the world offers, His peace remains undisturbed through every storm.

True joy, likewise, is not a passing emotion but a deep contentment found in God. *"You will show me the path of life. In your presence is fullness of joy. In your right hand there are pleasures forever more"* (Psalm 16:11). Joy in God's presence is undaunted by life's ups and downs. Even in suffering, it supports us, knowing our hope is secure in Him.

To live in this hope is to choose peace, even in chaos, a daily decision to focus not on struggles, but on God's faithfulness. When we fully trust Him, peace is no longer just a feeling, it becomes a way of life, an unshakable confidence that we are safe in His hands.

Joy, too, grows as we embrace God's love and sovereignty. It is not found in fleeting happiness but in Christ's unwavering presence. To live in this joy is to wake each day knowing our lives have meaning, we are deeply loved, and our future is secure in Him.

But the ultimate peace, the one that changes everything, comes in the moment of complete surrender, when our spirit is fully renewed in Christ. It is a peace beyond words, one that can only be understood by experiencing it. This is the fullness of

God's promise, the transformation that only true hope can bring.

Self-Reflection Activity:
- Are you truly experiencing the peace and joy that were promised earlier?
- Do you genuinely believe that such peace and joy can be attained from worldly pursuits?

Forgiveness: The Key to Freedom

God promises forgiveness to those who repent. *"If we confess our sins, he is faithful and righteous to forgive us the sins and to cleanse us from all unrighteousness"* (1 John 1:9). This assurance frees us from guilt, shame, and regret, offering a fresh start through His grace.

Forgiveness is not just about absolution; it is about healing and restoration. Isaiah 1:18 declares, *"Though your sins are as scarlet, they shall be as white as snow. Though they are red like crimson, they shall be as wool."* No failure is beyond God's mercy, and no past is beyond redemption.

Yet, to fully embrace this freedom, we must also forgive others. Jesus teaches in Matthew 6:14, *"For if you forgive men their trespasses, your heavenly Father will also forgive you."* Holding onto resentment only weighs us down. Forgiving does not mean excusing wrongs but choosing peace over bitterness and trusting God's justice.

Living in hope means embracing forgiveness daily, both receiving it and extending it. It is refusing to let past hurts define our future and walking in the freedom Christ provides. True hope gives us the strength to release pain, trust in God's justice, and experience deep, steadfast peace.

Forgiveness transforms us. It shifts our focus from pain to renewal, restores relationships, and fosters reconciliation. We are not bound by our past but continually renewed by God's love. To live in this hope is to carry a heart of mercy, extend grace as we have received it, and rest in the assurance that God's healing is complete, His justice is perfect, and His love never fails.

Self-Reflection Activity:
- Imagine you are speaking to a close friend who is struggling to forgive themselves. What advice would you give them? Now, apply that advice to yourself.
- How might embracing forgiveness, both giving and receiving, bring you greater freedom and peace in your life?
- What would it mean for you to trust in God's justice rather than carrying the burden of resentment on your own?

A Hope That Goes Beyond This Life

God promises eternal life to those who believe in Jesus Christ. *"For God so loved the world, that he gave his only born Son, that whoever believes in him should not perish, but have eternal life"* (John 3:16). This is the foundation of true hope, one that transcends the struggles of this world and reaches into eternity.

Unlike fleeting comforts, this hope is not based on achievements, wealth, or human effort but on God's unchanging love and grace.

Jesus reassures us, *"I give eternal life to them. They will never perish, and no one will snatch them out of my hand"* (John 10:28). No failure, trial, or external force can separate us from this promise. Nothing in all creation will be able to separate us from the love of God that is in Christ Jesus our Lord.

Living in this hope means shifting our focus from the temporary to the eternal. Our struggles are not the final word, *"For our light affliction, which is for the moment, works for us more and more exceedingly an eternal weight of glory,"* (2 Corinthians 4:17). This verse powerfully reminds us that our suffering is not without purpose, it is momentary and producing something far greater than we can now comprehend. Every trial, every hardship, is shaping us for an eternal glory that far outweighs our present pain. In this hope, we endure, knowing that what awaits us is beyond measure.

Rather than falling into despair during difficult times, we can trust that God arranges everything for the ultimate good of those who love Him and are aligned with His purpose. This assurance strengthens our resolve, encouraging us to persevere with confidence.

It calls us to let go of temporary attachments and firmly anchor ourselves in His unwavering promises.

Ultimately, to live in this hope is to wake each day with the confidence that our lives are held securely in His hands. It is not wishful thinking but a firm reality, anchored in God's unchanging love and the certainty of His eternal promise.

Self-Reflection Activity:
- Discuss with a friend or a mentor what it means to place hope in something eternal. How does their perspective challenge or affirm your own beliefs?
- What does it mean for you to trust in something greater than yourself when facing uncertainty and struggles?
- If eternal hope was real, how would it change the way you live, make decisions, and approach challenges today?

Sustained by God: Strength, Protection, and Victory

Life's trials test our endurance and reveal our weakness, yet God assures us we are never alone. He provides strength, protection, and victory over every obstacle.

"Yahweh is my strength and my shield. My heart has trusted in him, and I am helped. Therefore, my heart greatly rejoices. With my song I will thank him." (Psalm 28:7) His protection is constant, shielding those who trust in Him. Even in difficulty, we can walk with confidence, knowing His hand is upon us.

Beyond physical protection, God grants victory over sin, fear, and even death. *"But thanks be to God, who gives us the victory through our Lord Jesus Christ"* (1 Corinthians 15:57). This victory is not by our strength but through Christ, who has already overcome the world.

True strength comes from surrendering to God, not striving in our own power. *"He has said to me, 'My grace is sufficient for you, for my power is made perfect in weakness.' Most gladly therefore I will rather glory in my weaknesses, that the power of Christ may rest on me."* (2 Corinthians 12:9) In our weakest moments, He sustains us. Hardships are not signs of God's absence but opportunities to grow in faith, humility, and endurance.

"Yahweh will give strength to his people. Yahweh will bless his people with peace" (Psalm 29:11). God does not promise a life free from struggles, but He does promise to walk with us through them. His strength carries us when we cannot carry ourselves, and His peace steadies us in the storm.

I have experienced this firsthand. In a vision, while I was standing, a power suddenly came, lifted me into the sky, and carried me until I reached a church. That same power then returned me along the same path. God's message in this was clear: it was His strength alone that sustained me through the entire journey. Indeed, it had to be His power, because what I experienced would have been impossible for any human to endure. It was a vivid reminder that God's power is not limited by earthly constraints and that He is always at work.

In another vision, during a time of immense hardship, I saw an angel of the Lord carrying me above a storm that reached into the heavens. The storm below raged, but in His presence, there was peace. This vision reminded me that while endurance is necessary, it is God who ultimately sustains us. True hope is not about striving alone but yielding to His work, refining, upholding, and carrying us when we cannot stand.

True hope doesn't mean avoiding hardship, it means facing it with sureness, knowing the One who holds all things together is also holding us. Even when our strength fails, He remains unshaken. This truth changes everything for me personally; it reassures me that even when I fall short, God never will.

Self-Reflection Activity:
- Draw or create a visual representation of where your strength comes from in difficult times. What symbols, images, or words represent your source of strength?
- Have you ever experienced a moment when you realized a power beyond yourself was carrying you through?

- How would trusting in God's strength rather than your own change the way you face life's challenges?

Guidance for the Journey Ahead

Life is uncertain, but God is always with us. He not only charts our course but walks beside us, leading with wisdom, provision, and steadfast presence.

"But seek first God's Kingdom and his righteousness; and all these things will be given to you as well" (Matthew 6:33). When we put God first, He provides all we need. True guidance comes not from striving but from surrendering to Him.

"I will instruct you and teach you in the way which you shall go. I will counsel you with my eye on you" (Psalm 32:8). God's direction is personal and constant. I experienced this when I was unfairly terminated and faced a long season of unemployment. In isolation, God was drawing me closer. Through visions, He led me to pray and immerse myself in Scripture. What seemed like a setback was preparation, teaching me to rely fully on Him. His guidance is not just about direction but transformation.

Trust is key. *"Trust in Yahweh with all your heart, and don't lean on your own understanding. In all your ways acknowledge him, and he will make your paths straight."* (Proverbs 3:5-6). We often lean on our own plans, but true hope means surrendering control, trusting His wisdom above our own.

God's guidance sustains us, not just leads us. *"My God will supply every need of yours according to his riches in glory in Christ Jesus"* (Philippians 4:19). He equips us with strength, wisdom, and resources for the road ahead.

To live in this promise is to move forward in faith, not fear. Even when we cannot see the full picture, He does. Surrendering to His plan means stepping out with confidence, knowing His way is always greater.

Ultimately, embracing God's guidance frees us from wandering aimlessly. It anchors us in purpose, led by the One who sees the beginning and the end.

Self-Reflection Activity:
- In what areas of your life are you trying to rely on your own understanding instead of trusting God's guidance? Write them down
- How would fully surrendering your plans to God bring peace and clarity to your journey?
- Have you experienced a moment when God's provision or direction became clear in your life? How did it shape your faith?

Wisdom and Resilience in Uncertain Times

Life brings uncertainties and challenges that can leave us feeling overwhelmed, but God provides wisdom to navigate them and strength to persevere. He does not leave us to figure things out alone, He offers clarity, endurance, and guidance to those who trust Him.

"He gives power to the weak. He increases the strength of him who has no might" (Isaiah 40:29). When we are drained, emotionally, physically, or spiritually, God sustains us. *"I can do all things through Christ who

strengthens me" (Philippians 4:13). Our resilience is not from within but from Him.

God also grants wisdom to those who seek it. *"But if any of you lacks wisdom, let him ask of God, who gives to all liberally and without reproach, and it will be given to him"* (James 1:5). In times of uncertainty, His wisdom is always available to guide us.

Living in this promise means relying on God's wisdom rather than fear or confusion. Resilience is not about avoiding struggles but standing firm in faith, knowing God works all things for the good of those who love him.

When we embrace His wisdom and strength, we no longer walk in fear or doubt but with confidence, knowing He equips us to overcome every challenge.

Self-Reflection Activity:
- In times of uncertainty, do you find yourself relying on your own wisdom or seeking God's guidance?
- How have past challenges strengthened your faith and resilience?

- What steps can you take to trust God more fully in areas where you struggle with doubt or fear?

The Comfort of Knowing You're Never Alone

One of life's greatest assurances is that we are never truly alone. No matter the trial, God's presence is constant, offering comfort, strength, and peace.

"Even though I walk through the valley of the shadow of death, I will fear no evil, for you are with me. Your rod and your staff, they comfort me" (Psalm 23:4). His presence is not dependent on our circumstances, He remains with us through every high and low.

"Don't you be afraid, for I am with you. Don't be dismayed, for I am your God. I will strengthen you. Yes, I will help you. Yes, I will uphold you with the right hand of my righteousness." (Isaiah 41:10). There is no need to fear or be discouraged, for God is always present. He provides the strength we need in times of weakness, offering His help and unwavering support to uphold us with His righteousness.

I experienced this in a profound way during a time of extreme spiritual warfare. Overwhelmed and unable to hold myself together, I entered my prayer room, and in that moment, the entire atmosphere shifted. God's presence overtook the room, wrapping me in undeniable peace. It was as if He had come to console me, reminding me that I was not alone in the struggle.

Jesus reaffirmed this promise: *"Behold, I am with you always, even to the end of the age"* (Matthew 28:20). His presence is not temporary but eternal, guiding us every step of the way.

Living in this truth means facing challenges with courage, knowing we never bear them alone. It means surrendering fear and anxiety, replacing them with unshakable confidence in His faithfulness. When we fully embrace this reality, we find lasting peace, because we are never abandoned, never forsaken, and always held by His love.

Imagine a hope so secure that it does not rest on fleeting circumstances but on the unshakable foundation of Christ Himself. A hope rooted in everlasting love that never fades, peace and joy beyond understanding, salvation that promises eternal life, guidance and protection that never fail, and wisdom and resilience that strengthen us through life's greatest trials.

It is a hope that brings healing and restoration to the broken, strength and endurance in weakness, forgiveness that frees us from guilt and shame, and the constant presence of God, assuring us that He is always with us.

What kind of hope is this? It is the hope found in Jesus Christ, the only hope that never disappoints, the only hope that is eternal. Nothing in this world can offer all these things. Everything else fades, shifts, and crumbles, but the hope Christ offers remains steadfast.

To live in this hope is to walk in unshakable confidence, knowing we are fully known, deeply loved, and eternally secure in the hands of our Savior. This is the hope that heals, sustains, transforms, and leads us into the fullness of God's promise.

Self-Reflection Activity:

- Can you recall a time when you felt completely alone, yet looking back, you can see how God's presence was with you? How does this assurance change the way you face challenges today?

- Where is your hope anchored? Is it in temporary things that can fade, or in Christ, who offers everlasting love, peace, joy, and salvation?

- When life feels uncertain, do you find yourself trying to take control, or do you trust in God's guidance to lead you? What would it look like for you to fully surrender to His direction?

- Think of a time when you were at your weakest, physically, emotionally, or spiritually. How did God sustain you? How can you lean on His strength more instead of relying on your own?

- Is there an area in your life where you need healing, restoration, or forgiveness? How can you invite God to work in that space and bring His transforming grace?

Imagine a hope so secure that it does not rest on fleeting circumstances but on the unshakable foundation of Christ Himself. A hope that offers healing for the broken, peace in chaos, strength in weakness, and a future that is eternally secure.

Unlike the world's fragile, ever-changing promises, this hope does not shift with time, fail under pressure, or leave us empty. Everything else fades, wealth, success, relationships, even human strength, but the hope found in Jesus Christ remains steadfast. It is the only hope that never disappoints, the only hope that can sustain us through life and into eternity.

This hope doesn't just comfort, it transforms. It changes how we endure trials, how we make decisions, and how we trust in the unseen. It is not passive; it calls us to action, to live boldly in the truth of God's promises.

In the next chapter, we will explore what it means to put true hope into action, allowing it to shape our choices, fuel our faith, and lead us into a life fully surrendered to the One who is our eternal hope.

Chapter 4: True Hope in Action

True hope is a force that moves us forward, shaping our choices and guiding our actions. It is the bridge between believing in a better future and actively working toward it.

Let's explore how to cultivate true hope as a foundation, integrate it into daily life, overcome challenges, find strength in uncertain times, and surround ourselves with influences that reinforce hope. Let's dive into how we can live out true hope with purpose and intention.

Making True Hope a Lifelong Foundation

True hope is not something that comes and goes with circumstances. It is a foundation we build and strengthen over time. But like any foundation, it requires effort and intention to remain solid.

The first step to making hope a foundation in your life is to understand that it is a choice. Every day, you can choose to look for the good, to believe that better things are ahead, and to trust that God has a plan for your life.

Hope is not denial of reality; rather, it is seeing beyond current struggles to the promise of something greater.

Faith plays a critical role in sustaining hope. When we anchor our hope in Jesus, we are not simply relying on wishful thinking. We are standing on the promises of a faithful God.

Scripture reminds us in Jeremiah 29:11, "*For I know the thoughts that I think toward you," says Yahweh, "thoughts of peace, and not of evil, to give you hope and a future.*" When we build our hope on His word, we establish a foundation that withstands life's storms.

Building a foundation of hope also means adopting a long-term perspective. Too often, people lose hope when things don't change immediately. But just as a house takes time to be built brick by brick, hope is developed over a lifetime. We need to be patient with the process, trust that every experience has a purpose, and remind ourselves that God is always working behind the scenes.

Additionally, making hope a lifelong foundation means feeding it daily. Through prayer, scripture, gratitude, and choosing to trust even when things don't make sense. Hope grows when we practice it, live it, and share it with others. It is not passive; it is an active pursuit.

Daily Practices to Strengthen Hope

Hope is like a muscle; it grows stronger with consistent practice. By incorporating hope-filled habits into our daily routine, we reinforce a positive and faith-driven mindset.

Here are some practical ways to cultivate hope daily:

- Engaging with God's Word: The Bible is filled with hope-filled promises. Make it a habit to meditate on scripture that reminds you of God's faithfulness. Even just five minutes of reflection on a passage can bring strength to your day.

- Morning Reflections and Gratitude: Start your day by acknowledging the blessings in your life, no matter how small. Gratitude shifts your focus from what's lacking to what's present. Even on difficult days, finding just one thing to be thankful for can spark hope.

- Speaking Life Over Yourself: Our words carry power. Speak scripture, affirmations, and truths that reinforce hope. Remind yourself, *"I can do all things through Christ who strengthens me"* (Philippians 4:13). Instead of dwelling on problems, declare God's promises over your life.

- Acts of Kindness: Serving others fuels hope. When we bring hope to someone else, we are reminded of its power in our own lives. A simple word of encouragement, a small act of generosity, or being present for someone can uplift both the giver and the receiver.

- Journaling Hope: Writing down what you are believing for and how you see God working in your life can be an anchor in difficult times. Reviewing past entries can remind you of answered prayers and the progress you've made in your faith journey.

- Choosing Joy in Small Moments: Hope is often found in the little things, a laugh with a loved one, a beautiful sunset, or a quiet moment of reflection. Paying attention to these moments helps cultivate an attitude of expectancy and trust in God's goodness.

When hope becomes a part of your daily rhythm, it shapes your perspective and strengthens your ability to persevere. The more we practice hope, the more it becomes second nature to us, even in the face of challenges.

Overcoming Doubt and Setbacks

Even the most hope-filled person will face moments of doubt and discouragement. Life's challenges can make us question whether hope is worth holding onto. But overcoming doubt is a necessary part of deepening our trust in God's plan.

First, acknowledge your doubts without shame. Even great figures of faith wrestled with doubt. David frequently cried out to God in distress, as seen in Psalm 13:1-2: *"How long, Yahweh? Will you forget me forever? How long will you hide your face from me? How long shall I take counsel in my soul, having sorrow in my heart every day?"* Despite his doubts, David always turned back to trust in God's faithfulness (Psalm 13:5-6).

Likewise, Thomas the disciple struggled to believe in Jesus' resurrection, declaring, " *Unless I see in his hands the print of the nails, put my finger into the print of the nails, and put my hand into his side, I will not believe"* (John 20:25). Yet, Jesus did not condemn him but instead invited Thomas to see and believe (John 20:27).

Doubt and setbacks are not detours from God's plan; they are often part of it. God allows us to wrestle with uncertainty and hardship not to destroy our faith but to refine it. Since the fall of mankind, our nature has been prone to self-reliance, pride, and a desire for control. Through struggles, He gently draws us back, allowing us to see our deep need for Him.

True transformation doesn't happen in comfort; it happens in the refining fire of trials. Those who trust

Him through the process emerge stronger, not because they never doubted, but because they learned to depend on Him.

God does not reject us for our doubts; instead, He invites us to bring them to Him. As Jude 1:22 encourages, *"Be merciful to those who doubt."* Honest wrestling with faith leads to deeper trust, as we seek and find assurance in Him.

Second, remind yourself of past victories. Reflect on moments when God has come through for you before. Sometimes, looking back on His faithfulness is the fuel we need to keep moving forward. When facing setbacks, ask yourself: *Has God been faithful before?* If the answer is yes, then trust that He will be faithful again.

Third, stay connected to faith-filled voices. Doubt can thrive in isolation, but for many encouragement grows in community. Seek out mentors, faith groups, or trusted friends who will remind you of God's promises when your vision feels clouded. Often, hearing how God has restored hope in someone else's life can reignite the faith within your own heart.

Finally, take small steps of faith even when you don't feel hopeful. Action often reignites hope. Keep moving forward, even if it's one prayer, one scripture, or one act of trust at a time. Don't wait to feel hopeful before you act. Hope often comes through the very act of stepping forward.

Finding True Hope in Uncertain Times

Uncertainty is one of the greatest challenges to hope. When we don't know what's ahead, fear and anxiety can creep in. But hope does not require perfect circumstances, it thrives in the unknown.

One of the most powerful truths about hope is that it is not dependent on what we see but on what we believe. Hebrews 11:1 says, " *Now faith is assurance of things hoped for, proof of things not seen.*" When the future feels uncertain, we can hold onto the certainty of God's character.

Uncertain times test our faith, but they also present an opportunity to trust God in deeper ways. It is in the unknown that we develop resilience, patience, and a greater dependence on Him. The key is to shift our focus from what we don't know to what we do know, God is in control, He loves us, and He is always working for our good.

Rather than letting uncertainty lead to fear, let it push you closer to God. Pray more, seek Him more, and allow His peace to fill the gaps where answers are missing. Uncertainty may change our circumstances, but it does not have to steal our hope. With God, even the unknown is filled with possibility.

True Hope-Filled Influence

The people and messages we allow into our lives shape our perspective. If we surround ourselves with negativity, doubt, and fear, hope will struggle to thrive. But when we choose to immerse ourselves in an atmosphere of faith, encouragement, and positivity, hope flourishes.

Evaluate the voices in your life: friends, media, social circles. Are they feeding or draining your hope? Be cautious of influences that encourage false hope: those that promise transformation through quick fixes, material success, or shallow motivation without real substance. True hope is not based on illusions but on endurance, wisdom, and faith that stands the test of time.

Seek relationships that uplift and strengthen your spirit, encouraging you to grow in character rather than chase unrealistic ideals.

Hope is contagious, but so is deception. The more we surround ourselves with it, the more it becomes a natural part of our lives. Choose carefully what you allow to shape your perspective, ensuring that your hope is rooted in truth and not in empty promises.

Be intentional about creating a true hope-filled environment. Surround yourself with messages and teachings that inspire genuine transformation, rather than those that offer empty promises.

Engage deeply with scripture, allowing it to shape your perspective and guide your actions. Seek conversations that challenge and uplift you, rather than those that foster complacency or false assurances.

Be the kind of person who encourages others with wisdom and truth, and in doing so, you will find your own hope growing stronger and more deeply rooted.

Above all, pray for true hope, as it is the work of the Holy Spirit. True hope is a gift from God, nurtured through prayer and reliance on Him. Ask for the guidance and transformation that only the Holy Spirit can provide, and trust that genuine hope will take root in your life.

Self-Reflection Activity:

- In what areas of your life do you actively choose hope, and where do you struggle to maintain it? What small, intentional steps can you take to strengthen hope in your daily routine?

- Think about a recent challenge you faced. How would viewing it through the lens of true hope change the way you responded or felt about the situation?

- Hope is not passive; it requires practice. What daily habits (prayer, gratitude, speaking life, serving others) can you commit to in order to make hope a consistent foundation in your life?

- Hebrews 11:1 says, " Now faith is assurance of things hoped for, proof of things not seen." How do you typically respond when facing uncertainty? Do you allow fear to take control, or do you trust in God's unseen plan?

- The voices we surround ourselves with shape our hope. Who or what influences your perspective the most? Are these influences feeding your faith and hope, or are they leading you toward doubt and discouragement?

True hope is not just a concept; it is a reality that transforms lives. When we choose to live with true hope, we begin to see its power at work in our own journey and in the lives of others. In the next chapter, you will read three powerful stories of transformation. Real testimonies of individuals who have experienced the life-changing impact of hope in action. Let these stories inspire and remind you that no situation is beyond God's power to restore and renew.

Chapter 5: True Stories of Transformation

Transformation is the clearest evidence of true hope in action. Believing in hope is one thing, but witnessing lives transformed by it is another.

The following stories show how true hope moves people from despair to purpose, from setbacks to breakthroughs, and from uncertainty to renewed direction. These are real journeys of individuals who refused to give up and, in doing so, discovered profound transformation.

In my own testimony, however, I stumbled and even gave up at times. Yet, through God's grace, I found the strength to rise again, be renewed, and undergo my own transformation.

Overcoming Life's Hardest Moments

Transformation doesn't just happen despite hardships; it happens because of them. No one in biblical history underwent true transformation without facing trials. Hardship is not just an obstacle;

it is a spiritual necessity. Life often brings seasons of struggle, moments where everything seems lost and hope feels distant. Yet, history, faith, and personal testimonies reveal that it is in these very moments that transformation takes place.

Here are three powerful stories of people who overcame adversity through faith, perseverance, and the unwavering hope that carried them through.

A Personal Journey from Despair to Purpose

There was a time in my life when I felt completely lost, burdened by failures, uncertainty, and struggles that seemed impossible to overcome.

For nearly ten years, I suffered from PTSD, chronic anxiety, depression, and insomnia. These battles took a toll on my mind, emotions, and physical health, even disrupting my studies. Darkness clouded my dreams, and hope felt out of reach.

But in the depths of my suffering, I knew there had to be more. At the time, I was only attending a youth Bible study on some Friday nights, not because I had begun my journey of true hope, but because the youth group encouraged me to go. I was present, but my heart wasn't in it yet. That all changed when I truly surrendered to God. As I deepened my faith, I encountered a new battle: spiritual warfare. The closer I drew to Him, the fiercer the struggles became.

Just when I thought I had overcome one darkness, another phase of hardship began. After having children and relocating to a new state, I faced relentless challenges. Yet, amid these trials, something incredible happened.

The Holy Spirit constantly would assure me that my suffering was not meaningless, it was part of God's refining process. It wasn't punishment; but God's desire for my transformation. Still, the weight of my struggles often made me question God. How could He allow such suffering? There were times I couldn't see His love through the pain, and in my darkest moments, I felt abandoned. But even when I couldn't perceive Him, God was always present. My weakness was that I focused on my suffering rather than on His faithfulness.

Then, something remarkable happened, I started receiving dreams and visions of my spiritual battles before they unfolded. In these moments, I saw both the struggles ahead and the victories God had already won for me. These revelations reassured me that He was guiding my steps, even when I couldn't feel it.

Yet, PTSD, anxiety, depression, and relentless warfare still loomed over me, affecting every part of my life. But instead of being consumed by fear, I learned how to fight spiritually. Prayer became my refuge, fasting deepened my dependence on God, and immersing myself in Scripture reminded me of His promises. Each week, I found strength in the sacred rhythm of church services and holy sacraments, drawing closer to His presence. And in moments of deep exhaustion, I withdrew into spiritual retreats, seeking renewal and clarity.

God didn't simply pull me out of suffering, He transformed me through it. But in His mercy, whenever I reached my breaking point, He would give me rest.

With time, I've come to see those struggles weren't the end; they were the beginning of a transformation that reshaped every part of me. As I surrendered to God's refining process, my spiritual senses became heightened, making me more aware of His presence in ways I had never known before.

It was as if a veil had been lifted. I could truly say, *"I am in the Father, and the Father in me"* (John 14:11). A divine sensation of oneness with God filled my whole being, anchoring me in a peace beyond understanding.

Even my physical body was renewed, my skin felt like that of a newborn child, just as Job described his restoration: *"My flesh will be renewed like a child's; it will be restored as in the days of my youth"* (Job 33:25).

But the greatest transformation happened within my heart. My eyes were opened, and my heart was softened to the suffering of others. The words of Ezekiel became my reality: *" I will also give you a new heart, and I will put a new spirit within you. I will take away the stony heart out of your flesh, and I will give you a heart of flesh"* (Ezekiel 36:26). The burdens of others were no longer distant; their suffering deeply hurt me, as if it were my own. I was moved with compassion, feeling their pain and longing for God's mercy in their lives.

Through it all, an unshakable peace settled within me, calming my entire being. This was not a fleeting feeling; it was the very peace that Jesus promised: *"Peace I leave with you. My peace I give to you; not as the world gives, I give to you. Don't let your heart be troubled, neither let it be fearful."* (John 14:27).

I experienced this peace in greater heights when I was suffering, as if heaven and hell coexisted within me, the peace of God sustaining me while the pain of suffering raged on. Yet, His peace remained, guarding my heart and mind as I walked with Him.

There were other encounters too sacred to share, but what I can say with certainty is this: I am not the same person I once was. God did not merely bring me through the storm, He transformed me in the process.

Today, I walk in true hope, true peace, and true unity with Him. As His Word declares: *"Therefore if anyone is in Christ, he is a new creation. The old things have passed away. Behold, all things have become new"* (2 Corinthians 5:17).

Looking back, I now understand that what I received was more than just peace, it was true hope. A hope that is unshakable, rooted in faith, and anchored in God's promises, no matter what storms come my way.

The Story of Joseph: From Prisoner to Prince

The Bible gives us one of the most compelling examples of true hope and God's sovereign plan in the life of Joseph (Genesis 37-50). Betrayed by his own brothers, sold into slavery, and unjustly imprisoned, Joseph endured years of pain, isolation, and uncertainty.

Imagine the anguish, abandoned by the very people who were supposed to love him, left to navigate a foreign land as a slave. The betrayal alone could have shattered his spirit, but he chose faith over despair.

Even when falsely accused and thrown into prison for remaining pure before God, Joseph must have questioned his suffering. How could doing the right thing lead to such hardship? Did God see him? Was there a purpose in this pain?

Yet, even in his darkest moments, Joseph clung to faith. Though he surely wrestled with feelings of injustice and loneliness, he did not let them turn into bitterness. Instead, he remained steadfast, believing that God's plan would unfold in His perfect time.

One day, that time arrived.

God gave Pharaoh a troubling dream that no one could interpret, and it was in that moment that Joseph's years of suffering found their divine purpose. Brought from the depths of prison to the royal courts of Egypt, Joseph, through God-given wisdom, interpreted the dream, warning of an impending famine and providing a plan for Egypt's survival.

Recognising Joseph's God-given insight and leadership, Pharaoh appointed him as Egypt's second-in-command, with only Pharaoh himself holding greater authority. The very boy who had once been a slave and a prisoner now wore the robes of royalty, overseeing the nation's survival.

But the most astonishing part of Joseph's story wasn't just his rise to power, it was the fulfillment of the very dream he had shared with his family long ago. The dream that once made his brothers burn with jealousy was, in reality, God's revelation of his destiny.

When the famine struck, his brothers, the same ones who had betrayed him, came to Egypt seeking food, unknowingly bowing before the very man they had once sold into slavery.

In that moment, Joseph could have chosen revenge. Instead, he chose grace, acknowledging God's greater purpose in all his suffering. With tears in his eyes, he told his brothers, "You intended to harm me, but God intended it for good to accomplish what is now being done, the saving of many lives."

Joseph's story is a powerful reminder that hardships are not just random struggles, they are often divine preparations for something greater. His years of suffering were not wasted, they were the very means through which God positioned him to save countless lives, including his own family.

When we face trials, when we feel abandoned, when life seems unfair, we must remember Joseph's story. God is never absent, even in the darkest seasons. His plan is always in motion, shaping us, preparing us, and positioning us for something beyond what we can see.

Joseph's life teaches us that true hope is not in our circumstances, but in the God who controls them. No suffering is wasted in God's hands. If we trust Him, He will lead us, not just through the storm, but into the purpose He has destined for us.

A Modern Testimony of Overcoming Hardship

Life's trials can come in waves, each hardship seemingly more overwhelming than the last. For one individual, the journey of suffering began with the devastating loss of a beloved family member. Grief weighed heavily, leaving behind an emptiness that seemed impossible to fill.

As if that pain was not enough, a false accusation led to imprisonment for a crime that was never committed. Within those prison walls, suffering deepened. Torture, relentless trauma, and isolation became a daily reality. The weight of injustice pressed down, making hope seem like a distant illusion.

Upon release, the struggle did not immediately end. The wounds of the past lingered, shaping an internal battle that was just as difficult as the external hardships endured. Healing felt like a slow and painful process, but through it all, faith remained a guiding force.

Despite the darkness, this individual held onto faith in God with unshaken resolve. Church services became a refuge, scripture a source of strength, and acts of mercy a way to keep moving forward. Even in the midst of pain, prayers were lifted for others, interceding on behalf of those in need.

Through suffering, a deeper spiritual awareness emerged. As faith grew, moments of divine revelation followed, visions of the spiritual realm. Over time, these experiences refined the heart, revealing a greater reality beyond earthly struggles.

What was meant to break and destroy instead became a path of purification. Through endurance and unwavering hope, the pain of the past was transformed into a testimony of faith. Now, this life stands as a testament to God's redeeming power, a living reminder that even in unimaginable suffering, God is present, and hope is never lost.

This testimony, like so many others, is a powerful reminder that hope is not just a fleeting emotion. It is a force that sustains, transforms, and leads us through even the darkest trials. One person's unwavering hope can spark change, not only in their own life but in the lives of countless others. This is the power of one hopeful heart.

The Power of One Hopeful Heart

Hope is a powerful force. It has the ability to transform lives, break chains of despair, and ignite faith in those who feel lost. One person's unwavering hope can inspire change, not just in their own life, but in the lives of countless others. Throughout history, we see how hope: anchored in God has brought light into darkness, proving that even a single individual's trust in Him can alter the course of history.

The Hope of Abraham: A Legacy of Faith

Abraham's story is one of great hope. God called him to leave everything familiar and journey to an unknown land, with only a promise to hold onto, that he would become the father of many nations (Genesis 12:1-3). Despite his old age and Sarah's barrenness, Abraham believed. His hope in God's promise laid the foundation for the nation of Israel, demonstrating that faith-filled hope can lead to generations of blessings.

David's Hope Against Goliath

The young shepherd boy, David, stood before a giant that had an entire army paralysed with fear. What set him apart? Hope. While others saw defeat, David saw victory through God's power. He boldly declared, *"for the battle is Yahweh's"* (1 Samuel 17:47), and with one stone, he took down the giant. His unwavering hope not only secured his own victory but inspired a nation to trust in God's deliverance.

Jesus: The Ultimate Hope-Giver

The greatest example of hope transforming lives is found in Jesus Christ. When He walked the earth, He brought hope to the broken, the sick, the outcast, and the sinner. Through His death and resurrection, He not only demonstrated hope but became the source of eternal hope: offering salvation and reconciliation with God. Through His perfect obedience and sacrifice, He redeemed humanity, securing true hope for all who trust in Him.

How You Can Spread Hope Today

The impact of hope is not limited to biblical history. It is alive today in every heart that chooses to trust in God and share His love with others. One way I am sharing this hope with others is by writing this book. You can spread hope in simple but powerful ways:

- Speak life – Words of encouragement can uplift someone battling despair.

- Be present – Sometimes, just being there for someone makes all the difference.

- Share your testimony – Your story of hope can inspire others to trust in God.

- Pray for others – Interceding on someone's behalf brings God's power into their situation.

- Acts of kindness – Simple gestures like helping a neighbour, providing for the needy, or showing compassion can bring light to someone's day.

- Teach and mentor – Guiding others in faith, whether through formal teaching or everyday conversations, spreads the message of hope.

- Use your talents – Whether through music, art, writing, or service, you can inspire others by using your gifts to glorify God.

- Live with purpose – When we live with an awareness of God's calling, our lives become a testimony of His goodness. Let your actions reflect the hope you have received.

Never underestimate the power of hope. Just as Abraham, Job, David, and most importantly, Jesus, changed lives through hope, so can you. When one person chooses to hope in God and share that hope, ripples of transformation begin, touching lives in ways beyond imagination.

Will you be that person today?

Self-Reflection Activity:

- What promises from God am I holding onto, just as Abraham did? Consider the areas in your life where you are trusting God's plan, even when the outcome is uncertain.

- How can I demonstrate the kind of courageous hope that David had when facing Goliath? Identify challenges in your life where you need to rely on God's strength rather than your own.

- In what ways am I actively spreading hope to those around me? Beyond writing or sharing testimonies, how are you using your actions, words, and presence to encourage others?

- How can I grow in my understanding of Jesus as the ultimate hope-giver? Consider how Jesus' example influences your perspective on hope and how you can deepen your faith in His promises.

As you reflect on the promises you are holding onto, the challenges you are facing, and the ways you are sharing hope with others, remember that hope is not meant to remain a concept or a distant inspiration. It is an active, living faith that strengthens, sustains, and transforms.

Just as Abraham trusted God's promises, David relied on His strength, and Jesus embodied ultimate hope, you too are called to walk in hope daily. Even when the path is unclear, God is at work, shaping your journey.

As you step into the next chapter, open your heart to His guidance. True hope is a choice, a commitment to trust in the One who never fails.

Chapter 6: Your Hope Journey

Your Hope Reflections

Hope is a sacred journey that unfolds through life's challenges, victories, and seasons of searching. This section invites you to slow down, reflect intentionally, and capture how hope has formed, strengthened, and shaped your walk with God.

- What moments have strengthened your belief that something greater is ahead?
- When have you felt the deepest sense of despair, only to later see God's hand working behind the scenes?

True hope is a solid foundation rooted in the truth of God's promises. When we take time to look back on our lives, we begin to recognise patterns of grace, provision, and transformation. Even in the hardest of times, we can see how God has been moulding us, refining us, and leading us toward a deeper understanding of His purpose.

Reflect on your personal journey.

- What trials have tested your faith?
- When have you seen hope arise from the ashes of disappointment?
- Where have I seen God's faithfulness this year?
- What does it mean to me to live with unshakable hope?
- What practical change can I make this week to walk in hope?

Write down these moments as markers of God's faithfulness. They are stones of remembrance (Joshua 4:6–7), testifying to His goodness and reminding you that hope is not just about the future, it's about recognising His presence in every step of your journey. These reflections can become milestones of growth and reminders of God's grace as you continue to move forward.

When Hope Feels Hard

Hope can feel far away when you're walking through deep emotional pain. If you're experiencing depression, anxiety, or burnout, you may feel overwhelmed even by good things. Please know this: God sees you. He is not asking you to do everything; He invites you to begin with one small step.

Here are a few gentle ways to begin reconnecting with hope:

- Start with one small action: Choose just one meaningful thing today; read one verse, take a short prayer walk, or play a hymn. Small steps break through the heaviness and build momentum.

- Practice gentle self-compassion: Say to yourself, "I'm doing what I can today, and that's enough." Jesus is not disappointed in your weakness; He meets you in it.

- Stay grounded in the present: Pause and breathe deeply. Whisper: "Christ is with me now." Let that truth steady your heart.

- Reach out for support: Talk to a trusted friend, a spiritual father, or a professional Christian counsellor. You are not alone, and healing often begins with connection.

Remember: God loves you more than you can imagine. What you're walking through now will not last forever, He will turn your trial into testimony. One day, you will proclaim His goodness with joy. Start with one small act of faith, repeated gently each day, trusting that God is walking with you, even when you can't feel Him.

Identifying & Letting Go of False Hope

In a world that constantly offers temporary solutions, many things promise hope but leave us empty. While they offer temporary satisfaction, they can never truly anchor the soul.

- What false hopes have you clung to in the past?

Maybe it was the expectation that a new job, a different city, good health, or a particular relationship would bring peace. Perhaps it was the thought that once a certain problem was solved, everything else would fall into place. But as time passed, you realised these things did not provide the deep, unshakable hope your heart longed for.

Letting go of false hope requires surrender, laying down our own plans, desires, and expectations at the feet of Jesus Christ and trusting Him to be our true source of hope. It means realising that nothing in this world can compare to the security found in Him. As you reflect on this, ask yourself:

- What am I holding onto that is preventing me from experiencing the fullness of true hope?

If you are not a believer in Jesus Christ or have drifted away from faith, take a moment to reflect on what is keeping you from trusting in Him.

True and lasting hope is only found in Christ. Without taking the first step of believing in and accepting Jesus, it is impossible to obtain and fully experience the transformative power of true hope. Be courageous, surrender those burdens to God, and embrace the assurance that His plans are always greater, wiser, and filled with a hope that never fails.

Staying Anchored in True Hope Through Challenges

Life's storms are inevitable. Difficulties come in many forms, health issues, financial struggles, loss, disappointment, or seasons of waiting. In those moments, hope can feel fragile, like a flickering flame in the wind. But true hope is not easily extinguished. When rooted in God, it becomes an anchor that holds firm, no matter the waves that crash against us.

Here are strategies to stay anchored:

- Hold onto God's promises. His Word is filled with assurances that He is with us, for us, and working all things for our good. Meditate on scriptures that remind you of His faithfulness.

- Pray with expectation. Prayer is not just about asking, it is about surrendering and trusting. Pour out your heart to God and allow Him to strengthen your spirit.

- Surround yourself with truth. The voices we listen to shape our perspective. Choose to surround yourself with people, messages, and teachings that reinforce faith, not fear.

- Keep moving forward. Even when progress feels slow, continue taking steps of faith and obedience. Hope grows as we choose to trust God, one step at a time, even when the path isn't clear.

There may be moments when you feel completely abandoned, lose hope, and actually give up on God and everything connected to Him. But remember, God will renew your spirit. He will restore you to the place you once had with Him, and through it all, He will teach you humility in a way nothing else can.

These experiences strip us of pride, reminding us that we are truly nothing without Him, and that we live and move only by His grace. It's a priceless lesson; one that can only be learned through such trials; which is why God, in His wisdom, allows them as part of our journey of transformation.

If you find yourself unable to hold onto hope, cry out to God:

> *"Lord, you can see me, my emotions, and my struggles. Please help me, have mercy on me, and give me the assurance that You are with me."*

Say the prayer with humility and faith, and you will be helped and assured. Even if you falter, He will not fail you. His promise to those who believe in Him is unshakable, He must bring you through, for He is faithful to His word.

I know this firsthand; no matter how great my fall or weakness, He has always been faithful, never once has He withheld His merciful hands from me. Take this to heart, true hope is more than a passing feeling or mere optimism. It is a precious gift from God, received when you place your trust in Him and endure by His grace.

This hope is not dependent on your circumstances; it does not waver with the ups and downs of life. Instead, it is deeply rooted in God's unwavering faithfulness, bringing true joy and peace that the world cannot offer.

Your part in this? Trust Him. Place your faith in Him, even when you don't understand the journey. And when you do, He will do His part, filling you with a hope so powerful that it overflows into every part of your life. This hope is not something you merely hold onto; it is something that holds onto you.

So, trust Him. Let His hope anchors you, steady you, and remind you that He is always with you, working in you through the power of the Holy Spirit.

Hope Practices Toolbox

True hope must be lived out. Here are practical ways to apply it daily:

- Daily Scripture Meditation: Choose one verse a week and spend time each day meditating on it and bringing it to God in prayer.

- Hope Journal: Record moments of God's faithfulness.

- Hymns and Praises: Enrich your spirit with hymns, psalms, and praises that draw you closer to God.

- Hope Partner: Walk with someone who encourages your faith.

- Monthly Reflection: Take time to revisit your journey and notice growth.

A Three-Step Action Plan

These three steps will help you move forward in faith, no matter where you are in your journey:

Step 1: Anchor Your Hope in Something Unshakable

- Reflect on where your hope is placed.

- Write a personal hope statement based on a bible verse (e.g., Romans 15:13).

Step 2: Let Go of What Holds You Back

- Identify fears or doubts and surrender them to God in prayer.

- Replace false hopes with biblical truths:

  - Wealth will save me ➜ *"Do not store up for yourselves treasures on earth..."* (Matthew 6:19-21)

  - Health will guarantee peace ➜ *"My grace is sufficient for you..."* (2 Corinthians 12:9)

  - Relationships will complete me ➜ *"You are complete in Him..."* (Colossians 2:10)

  - Success will bring meaning ➜ *"What good is it for someone to gain the whole world..."* (Mark 8:36)

- Consider practicing a spiritual discipline such as fasting, particularly during a period of surrender. Fasting humbles the soul and helps you focus on God above all else.

- Practice confession and repentance. Sometimes what holds us back is unaddressed sin or lingering shame. Bring it before God in prayer and spiritual confession. His forgiveness restores joy and renews strength. *"If we confess our sins, he is faithful and righteous to forgive us the sins, and to cleanse us from all unrighteousness."* (1 John 1:9).

- Seek spiritual guidance: Letting go often requires outside perspective. Speak with a spiritual father, mentor, or spiritually mature believer who can help you discern God's truth and lead you in surrender. God often brings clarity and freedom through Godly counsel.

- Pray a prayer of release:

"O Lord Jesus Christ, I lay down every false hope and broken trust at Your feet. Teach me to renounce all that draws my heart away from You. Grant me the grace to surrender my will to Yours, that I may walk in humility and peace. Fill me with the true hope that is born from Your Resurrection and sustained by Your mercy. Strengthen me, O Lord, to rely only on Your divine providence, now and forever. Amen."

Step 3: Take a Step of Faith Today

Step 3: Take a Step of Faith Today

- Commit to one act of faith: pray, study the Word, join a Bible study group, serve someone in need, speak hope and encouragement, or give financially to ignite hope in someone's life.

- If you're ready to follow Christ, pray a prayer of surrender (found in the following pages) and ask Him to transform your heart and life.

Walking Forward with Confidence

Hope gives us the courage to move forward. It is not just about enduring the present but stepping boldly into the future with confidence, knowing that God is guiding our steps. Walking forward in hope means trusting that even when the path is unclear, He is leading the way.

This is your journey. Every moment of growth, every lesson learned, every challenge overcome has brought you to this point. Now, it is time to walk forward, not with fear, but with faith. Keep your eyes fixed on Jesus Christ, the author and perfecter of your faith. His hope is your foundation, your strength, and your future.

No matter what lies ahead, remember this, If your hope is based on Jesus Christ, then your hope is real. It is alive. It is unshakable. And it will carry you through every step of your journey.

Where to Next?

You may be wondering: *What comes after this book? How do you continue this journey of hope?*

Here are four ways to keep growing:

1. Deepen Your Journey with the 30-Day Devotional Companion

   If you're longing to keep growing in hope day by day, "Living in True Hope – A 30-Day Journey of Faith and Renewal" may be just the next step. It's not just more reading, it's a guided experience with Scripture, prayer, and gentle action steps to help you live out what you've discovered. You'll also find space for journaling and a simple activation plan to bring hope in every part of your life. *Visit the website & go to 'Books' to access this book.*

2. Share the Message of Hope

   Hope grows when it's shared. One of the most powerful ways to strengthen your own hope is by encouraging someone else. When Christ was in pain on the cross, He looked beyond His own agony and cared for those around Him (John 19:26-27). Whether it's sharing this book, offering a kind word, or praying for someone who's struggling, your act of love may be the spark of hope someone desperately needs. And in giving, you'll find your own hope renewed.

3. Reflect and Grow with the Online Course

   If you're ready to apply these truths in practical ways, the *Applied True Hope* course offers space to slow down and reflect more deeply. Whether you've read this book, the devotional, or you're starting fresh, the course brings the same core themes to life through personal reflection, guided exercises, and spiritual insights to help you live anchored in Christ—day by day. *Visit the website & go to 'Courses' to access the online course.*

4. Stay Rooted in the Practice

The journey of hope is lifelong. Keep watering the seeds God has planted by:

- Staying in prayer and Scripture
- Journaling your journey with God
- Staying connected to a Christ-centered community.

These small, faithful practices will continue to anchor you when life feels uncertain.

True hope is not the end of your story. It is the beginning of a new one. The invitation is open. Will you take the next step of faith? *"May the God of hope fill you with all joy and peace as you trust in Him, so that you may overflow with hope by the power of the Holy Spirit"* Romans 15:13. This is your journey. Walk in it boldly. Let hope lead the way.

Conclusion

Key Takeaways from This Journey

- *Hope in temporary things is unreliable* – Success, relationships, wealth, and achievements may provide comfort, but they cannot sustain us. True hope must be anchored in something unshakable.

- *False hope leads to disappointment* – Many people chase illusions that fail to bring fulfillment. Recognising and letting go of false hopes is the first step toward real transformation.

- *True hope is found in Jesus Christ* – Unlike worldly hope, which is uncertain, hope in Christ is unwavering, constant, and available to all who seek Him.

- *True hope is a choice* – Choosing to trust God, surrender fears, and embrace His promises transforms how we face life's uncertainties.

- ***True hope is active, not passive*** – It shapes our daily actions, gives us peace in challenges, and strengthens us when we feel weak.

- ***Forgiveness and letting go bring freedom*** – Holding onto past hurts and disappointments can block us from experiencing true hope. True hope allows us to move forward unburdened.

- ***God's love is steadfast*** – Nothing can separate us from His love. When we anchor our hope in Him, we can walk in confidence and security.

- ***Living in true hope gives us purpose*** – Hope is not just for personal comfort; it calls us to action. We are meant to walk in faith, share hope with others, and trust in God's greater plan.

- ***True hope extends beyond this life*** – The ultimate promise of hope is eternal life in Christ, giving us peace and confidence in all circumstances.

Living with Purpose and Confidence

This journey has revealed that true hope is a strong foundation. It does not depend on circumstances but on a truth that never changes, God is in control, His promises are sure, and His love is eternal. When we live in this hope:

- We walk in faith rather than fear.
- We trust God's plan even when life is uncertain.
- We find strength in trials rather than being overcome by them.
- We let go of the past and move forward in freedom.
- We share this hope with others who are searching.

Choosing to live in true hope does not mean we will never face difficulties. But it does mean that we are never without purpose, never without guidance and never without a future.

Step Into True Hope

Hope is more than a comforting thought; it is the foundation of a transformed life. A life without Christ leads to fear, despair, and instability. But in Him, there is peace, healing, and eternal security.

If you've ever felt overwhelmed by fear, weighed down by anxiety, or burdened by hopelessness, know this: Jesus Christ is the true hope you've been searching for. He alone provides a hope that never fades, a peace that surpasses understanding, and a joy that sustains even in the darkest moments.

I know this because I have lived it. For years, I battled PTSD, chronic anxiety, depression, and insomnia, a constant war within my mind and body. My struggles affected not just my emotions but also my physical and spiritual well-being. I tried to find relief in different ways, yet nothing brought lasting peace.

It wasn't until I chose to live a life of daily surrender to Christ that I experienced the kind of healing no human effort could provide. His hope didn't just comfort me, it transformed me, restoring my mind, body, and spirit.

Maybe you've felt like something was missing, as if no achievement, success, or effort could truly satisfy or bring the healing your heart longs for. Perhaps you've battled anxiety, depression, or the weight of physical and emotional struggles, wondering if peace is even possible. If so, you're not alone. That longing for something deeper, for true restoration, is woven into every heart. But the search doesn't have to continue.

Christ has been calling you all along. His hope is real. His love is unwavering. His promises never fail.

If you are searching for something lasting, Jesus is the answer. He alone offers a peace that endures, a love that restores, and a future that is secure.

He is ready to transform your life. Will you let Him? If you're ready to embrace this hope, open your heart to Him today and let these words be your prayer of surrender.

Prayer of Surrender

O Lord, Almighty and Everlasting God, I come before You in humility, longing for a hope that never fades. You are the Fountain of Life, the Light that pierces darkness, and the refuge for my weary soul.

I have searched for hope in the world but found nothing lasting. My heart remains restless despite all I have pursued. Today, I turn from false hopes and surrender fully to You: my only true and eternal hope.

Lord Jesus Christ, Son of the Living God, have mercy on me, a sinner. In Your infinite love, You bore my sins so that I might receive life and salvation. Wash me, cleanse me, and make me new. I renounce all that has kept me from You and open my heart to receive You as my Lord and Savior.

Come, O Christ, and dwell within me. Shine Your light into the depths of my soul. Strengthen me in weakness, renew my faith, and anchor me in the certainty of Your promises. Fill me with Your Holy Spirit, that I may live not in fear but in the confidence of Your unfailing love.

Teach me to trust You completely, to walk in righteousness, and to rest in the assurance that You are always with me. Be my refuge in trials, my peace in storms, and my joy in all seasons. From this moment on, I place my hope in You alone.

For You alone are the Alpha and Omega, the King of kings, and the Lord of all. In You, my hope is whole, and my future secure.

To You be all glory, honour, and worship, now and forever. Amen.

If you have prayed this prayer, know that you are not alone. Heaven rejoices over you, and God's love surrounds you. As you begin this new journey, allow this prayer to strengthen and encourage your heart.

My Prayer for You

O my Lord Jesus Christ, the source of all hope, I lift up this reader before You. You know their heart, their burdens, and their longing for peace. Strengthen them in faith, guide them in truth, and fill them with the light of Your presence.

When doubt arises, be their assurance. When fear surrounds them, be their refuge. Let them walk in the confidence of Your love, knowing they are never alone. Anchor their soul in the unshakable hope found in You alone. May they trust You fully, live in Your peace, and shine as a light to others.

To You be all glory, now and forever. Amen.

Next Steps: Continue seeking God daily. Spend time in His Word, speak to Him in prayer, and surround yourself with others who will encourage your faith. Remember, hope in Christ is not just for today—it is for eternity.

Want to go deeper in your journey? Explore bonus content, exclusive downloads, and more at www.brimlightpress.com

My Hope Commitment

Today, I choose to anchor my life in the true and unshakable hope found in Jesus Christ.

I commit to walk in faith, release false hopes, and trust in His promises.

I may not have all the answers, but I believe that Christ holds my future and walks with me each step of the way.

Signed: _____

Date: _____

"This hope we have as an anchor of the soul, a hope both sure and steadfast and entering into that which is within the veil."

Hebrews 6:19

About the Author

I have spent years in human services, walking alongside individuals and families through challenges. I have also worked in vocational education and training, equipping people with the skills to create meaningful change. Yet, through it all, I have seen a deeper need: people searching for true hope but often looking in the wrong places.

True hope is essential, yet many struggle to find it in the one source that never fails. I have witnessed how misplaced hope, whether in quick fixes or self-reliance, leaves people weary and unfulfilled.

My heart's desire is to help others discover the unshakable, eternal hope found only in Jesus Christ. This book is a guide to that path, a call to seek the hope that truly changes lives. My prayer is that this message blesses you and inspires you to share it, allowing true hope to multiply in the lives of those around you.

With hope in Christ,

Robel Teklom

www.ingramcontent.com/pod-product-compliance
Lightning Source LLC
Chambersburg PA
CBHW031255290426
44109CB00012B/584